SPANISH 1
LIFEPAC NIN[E]

CONTENTS

I.   **HISPANIC TOWN SQUARE** 2

II.   **CONVERSATION & INDIRECT OBJECT PRONOUNS** 9

III.   **IN THE CLASSROOM, USING OBJECT PRONOUNS** 15

IV.   **PREPOSITIONAL PRONOUNS** 20

V.   **REVIEW AND USE OF IDIOMS** 25

VI.   **CULTURE: LIFE IN SPAIN** 30

VII.   **COMPREHENSION, WRITING AND CONVERSATION** 35

VIII.   **REVIEW AND COMPARISONS** 39

     VOCABULARY LIST 42

Author: **Vicki Seeley Milunich, B.A., M.S. Ed.**
Editor: Alan Christopherson, M.S.
Graphic Design: Kyle Bennett, Jennifer Davis,
                 Alpha Omega Staff

Alpha Omega Publications

Published by Alpha Omega Publications, Inc.
300 North McKemy Avenue, Chandler, Arizona 85226-2618

SPANISH 1: LIFEPAC NINE
UN PUEBLO TÍPICO

OBJECTIVES

When you have completed this LIFEPAC, you should be able to:

1. Introduce the vocabulary specific to small town life in a Hispanic country.

2. Explain indirect object pronouns, their use and placement in the sentence.

3. Explain the use of both direct and indirect object pronouns together in one sentence.

4. Introduce certain idioms using prepositions.

5. Explain the culture of Spain with specific reference to small town life.

6. Review material previously learned in LIFEPAC 8.

1

I. HISPANIC TOWN SQUARE

Conversación – Vamos al pueblo

Mario:	¿Quieres ir al centro conmigo?
Carlota:	Sí. ¿Qué necesitas?
Mario:	Mi madre necesita unas cosas. Me pidió ir por ella.
Carlota:	Voy a preguntarle a mi madre si ella necesita unas cosas también.
Mario:	Bueno. Voy a esperarte en mi casa.
Carlota:	Hola. Estoy lista.
Mario:	¡Qué bueno! Tengo que ir a la carnicería, la panadería, la pastelería y por supuesto la heladería.
Carlota:	Bien. Tengo que ir a la panadería también y la dulcería y la papelería.
Mario:	Me gusta nuestro pueblo.
Carlota:	Las tiendas pequeñas me encantan mucho.
Mario:	El Sr. Gomez es un carnicero excelente. Me gusta la carne de su carnicería.
Carlota:	Y la Sra. Cisneros hace los mejores dulces del mundo.
Mario:	Tienes razón. Y el pan de la panadería es siempre delicioso.
Carlota:	Tenemos suerte de vivir en este pueblo.
Mario:	Estoy de acuerdo contigo en eso.

Translation – Let's go to town

Mario:	Do you want to go downtown with me?
Carlota:	Yes. What do you need?
Mario:	My mother needs some things. She asked me to go for her.
Carlota:	I am going to ask my mother if she needs some things also.

Mario:	Good. I am going to wait for you at my house.
Carlota:	Hi. I'm ready.
Mario:	Great! I have to go to the butcher shop, the bakery, the pastry shop and, of course, the ice cream shop.
Carlota:	Fine. I have to go to the bread store, too, and the candy shop and the stationery shop.
Mario:	I like our town.
Carlota:	I love our small shops.
Mario:	Mr. Gomez is an excellent butcher. I like the meat from his butcher shop.
Carlota:	And Mrs. Cisneros makes the best candies in the world.
Mario:	The bread from the bakery is always delicious.
Carlota:	We are lucky to live in this town.
Mario:	I have to agree with you on that.

Look at the conversation and write the meanings of the following words or phrases.

1.1

a. al centro _____

b. unas cosas _____

c. me preguntó _____

d. esperarte _____

e. la carnicería _____

f. la panadería _____

g. la pastelería _____

h. la papelería _____

i. un carnicero _____

j. la carne _____

k. las mejores dulces _____

l. del mundo _____

m. tenemos suerte _____

n. estar de acuerdo _____

o. contigo _____

Conversation Practice

1.2   Practice the conversation above with your learning partner so that you may say it without looking at the text.

✔ Adult check _____

Initial   Date

Vocabulario: El pueblo

la carnicería	the butcher shop	**el carnicero**	the butcher
la dulcería	the candy shop	**el dulcero**	the confectioner
la farmacia	the pharmacy	**el farmacéutico**	the pharmacist
la florería	the flower shop	**el florero**	the florist
la frutería	the fruit store	**el frutero**	the fruit vendor
la heladería	the ice cream shop	**helar (ie)**	to freeze
la lechería	the dairy store	**el lechero**	the milkman
la librería	the book store	**el librero**	the book vendor
el mercado	the market	**el mercadero**	the merchant
la panadería	the bakery	**el panadero**	the baker
la papelería	the stationery shop	**el papelero**	the paper merchant
la pastelería	the pastry shop	**el pastelero**	the pastry chef
la zapatería	the shoe store	**el zapatero**	the shoe maker

Note that the above vocabulary shows the relationship of word families. These are words that are related in meaning. We have the same concept in English – the cook cooks, the wrestler wrestles in the wrestling match. There are also feminine forms of the people: **la panadera, la zapatera, la lechera**.

Ejercicio.

1.3   Look at the following products and write the store where they are sold and the vendors who sold them. Refer to the vocabulary list above.

a. el libro   _____   _____

b. la carne   _____   _____

c. el pastel   _____   _____

d. los zapatos   _____   _____

e. el pan   _____   _____

f. la leche   _____   _____

g. las frutas   _____   _____

h. los dulces   _____   _____

i. las flores   _____   _____

j. el papel   _____   _____

Fill in the blank with a word from the vocabulary on page 4 that best completes the sentence.

1.4

    a. El Sr. Chavez vende frutas porque es _____.

    b. Tengo que ir a _____ para comprar flores.

    c. Estoy enfermo. Voy a _____ por las medicinas.

    d. Necesito comida para sandwiches. Voy a _____.

    e. Quiero unos dulces. Voy en _____.

    f. El Sr. Ayala es librero en _____.

    g. Voy a comprar _____ en la zapatería.

    h. La pastelería tiene _____ deliciosos.

    i. Necesito los cuadernos y el papel, entonces voy a _____.

    j. Compramos queso, leche y mantequilla en _____.

Identify the store where the following items would be bought and write it underneath the picture.

a. _____   b. _____

c. _____   d. _____   e. _____

f. _____   g. _____   h. _____

i. _____   j. _____

SELF TEST 1

1.01 **Write the name of the shop in Spanish on the line.** (5 pts. each)

a. _____

b. _____

c. _____

d. _____

e. _____

f. _____

g. _____

h. _____

i. _____

j. _____

1.02   **Write the names of the persons who work in the stores shown on the previous page.** (5 pts. each)

a. _____   f. _____

b. _____   g. _____

c. _____   h. _____

d. _____   i. _____

e. _____   j. _____

Score _____

Teacher check _____
              Initial   Date

II. CONVERSATION & INDIRECT OBJECT PRONOUNS

Conversación – ¿A quién?

Victor:	Tengo que ir al mercado para mi mamá.
Gerardo:	¿Por qué?
Victor:	Le prometí a ella.
Gerardo:	¿Qué va a comprarle?
Victor:	Necesita unas cosas. Tengo una lista que me dio.
Gerardo:	Puedo acompañarte.
Victor:	Gracias.
Gerardo:	Necesito recordar comprar dulces.
Victor:	¿Para quién?
Gerardo:	Para mis hermanitas. Siempre les compro algo cuando voy.
Victor:	Eres un hermano magnífico.
Gerardo:	No me hace bromas.
Victor:	No, es verdad.
Gerardo:	Vamos ahora.

Translation – To whom?

Victor:	I have to go to the market for my mom.
Gerardo:	Why?
Victor:	I promised her.
Gerardo:	What are you going to buy for her?
Victor:	She needs some things. I have a list she gave me.
Gerardo:	I can go with you.
Victor:	Thanks.
Gerardo:	I need to remember to buy candy.
Victor:	For whom?
Gerardo:	For my little sisters. I always buy them something when I go.
Victor:	You are a great brother.
Gerardo:	Don't pick on me.
Victor:	No, it's true.
Gerardo:	Let's go now.

Ejercicio.

2.1   Refer to the above conversation and identify the meaning of the following bolded words.

a. **Le** prometí **a ella**. _____

b. ¿Qué va compararle **le** _____

c. accompañar**te** _____

d. Siempre **les** compro _____

e. No **me** haces bromas. _____

Indirect Object Pronouns

The indirect object pronouns are pronouns which take the place of the indirect object. As with the direct object pronouns they are placed directly in front of the conjugated verb, attached to the infinitive (**-ar, -er, -ir**) or present participle (**-ando, -iendo**).

The indirect object is the word in the sentence that answers the question "To/for whom/what is the action being done?" The person or object is indirectly benefiting from the action of the verb. (This is in contrast to the direct object which is being acted directly upon – "Who/what receives the action?")

Examples:

I give Paul his paper.
Who/what is receiving the action of giving – the paper – direct object.
To/for whom is it being given – Paul – indirect object.

Ann writes me a letter.
Who/what is receiving the action of writing – the letter – direct object.
To/for whom is it being written – me – indirect object.

We bring the work to the teacher.
Who/what is receiving the action of bringing – the work – direct object.
To/for him is it being brought – the teacher – indirect object.

The indirect object pronouns are:

	Singular		**Plural**
me	to/for me	**nos**	to/for us
te	to/for you (fam)	**os**	to/for you (fam. Spain)
le	to you, to him, to her	**les**	to you, to them

Rules:

1. The forms of **le** and **les** are used for both masculine and feminine objects.
2. Since **le** and **les** can mean so many different forms, it is often clarified by adding **a él, a ella, a Ud.** to **le**, or **a ellos, a ellas, a Uds.** to **les**.

Examples: **Les digo la verdad a ellos.**   I tell them the truth.
Le traigo las bebidas a Ud.   I am bringing you the drinks.

3. Note that in English the "to" may be stated or implied. "He writes a letter to me every day," or "He writes me a letter every day."
4. Note that the **me, te, nos, os** forms are the same as those for direct object pronouns and reflexive pronouns.
5. Placement:
   Before the conjugated verb: **Maria le da a él el dinero.**
   Attached to the infinitive: **Voy a traerles las bebidas.**
   Attached to the present participle: **Estás devolviéndonos los regalos.**

Write the English translation of the following sentences.

2.2
a. Paco me trae un libro. _____

b. Le compro a él un refresco. _____

c. Tengo que darte las noticias. _____

d. Les venden a ellos el coche. _____

e. Nos ofreces un regalo. _____

f. Le prestes a ella su coche. _____

g. Nos prometen llegar a tiempo. _____

h. Te anunciamos el premio. _____

i. La madre les sirve a ellos la comida. _____

j. El profesor les devuelve a Uds. la tarea. _____

k. Están mostrándonos las fotos. _____

l. Tengo que darte este papel. _____

m. Estamos vendiéndoles la casa. _____

n. Puedes servirles el té. _____

o. Estás explicándome la lección. _____

Rewrite the sentence, replacing the underlined word with an indirect object pronoun and placing it correctly in the sentence.

Example: Pedro compra unos dulces <u>para Maria.</u>
Pedro le compra a ella unos dulces.

2.3
a. Luis vende su auto <u>a Miguel.</u> _____

b. Doy las gracias <u>a mis amigos.</u> _____

c. Describimos el viaje <u>a los estudiantes.</u> _____

d. No dice el secreto <u>a mi hermana.</u> _____

e. El padre lee un cuento <u>a su hijo.</u> _____

f. Estamos mostrando la carta <u>a nuestros amigos.</u> _____

g. Tenemos que dar las frutas <u>a mamá.</u> _____

h. Deseo servir la cena <u>a los huespuedes (guests)</u> a las ocho.

_____

i. Ofrezco ocho dolares <u>a Luis.</u> _____

j. La clase canta la canción <u>a sus padres.</u> _____

Answer the following questions using an indirect object pronoun in your answer.

Example: ¿Dónde va a dar el regalo a Mariana?
Voy a darle el regalo a su casa.

2.4

a. ¿Qué muestras a tus amigos?

b. ¿Para qué compran Uds. los regalos para Ana?

c. ¿Cuánto dinero presta Ud. a su hijo?

d. ¿Cuándo vas a dar las noticias a tu amiga?

e ¿Cuál suéter das a tu hermana?

Te toca a ti.

Prepare a conversation using the following guidelines. You and a friend are discussing Christmas gifts.

2.5

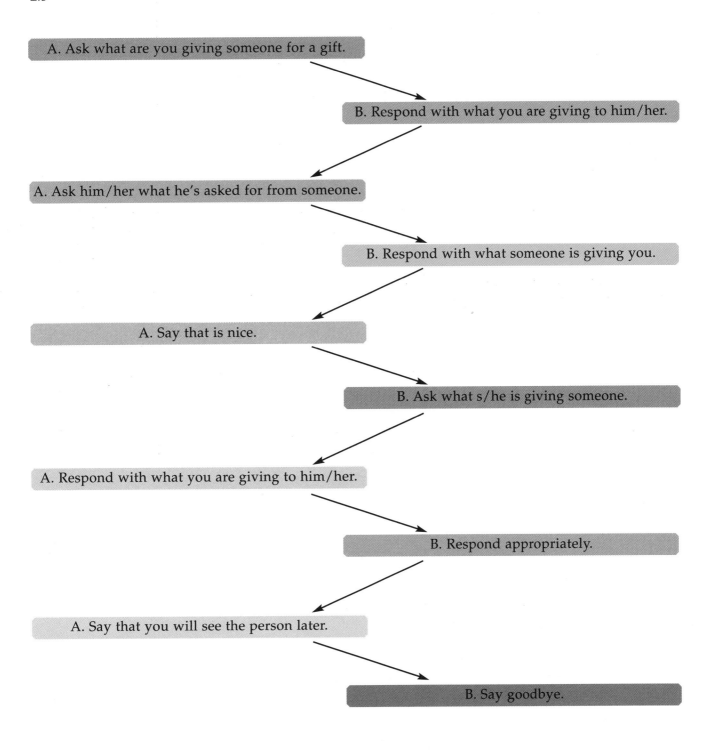

A. Ask what are you giving someone for a gift.

B. Respond with what you are giving to him/her.

A. Ask him/her what he's asked for from someone.

B. Respond with what someone is giving you.

A. Say that is nice.

B. Ask what s/he is giving someone.

A. Respond with what you are giving to him/her.

B. Respond appropriately.

A. Say that you will see the person later.

B. Say goodbye.

✔ Adult check _____

Initial   Date

SELF TEST 2

2.01 **Rewrite the following sentences using the indirect object pronoun instead of the indirect object.** (10 pts. each)

a. Mario compra seis billetes para sus amigos.

b. Uds. muestran sus buenas notas a sus padres.

c. Devuelves los libros a su tía.

d. La profesora enseña la lección a sus alumnos.

e. Ofrezco diez dolares al Sr. Lopez por su silla vieja.

2.02 **Translate the following to English.** (10 pts. each)

a. Arturo me presta veinte dolares.

b. La clase nos presenta el trabajo de Mark Twain.

c. Te traigo tres botellas de leche.

d. Tengo que darte un examen.

e. Están escribiéndonos una carta.

80 / 100

Score _____

Teacher check _____
                Initial   Date

III. IN THE CLASSROOM, USING OBJECT PRONOUNS

Conversación - Una decepción

David: Tengo que escribir una carta a nuestra abuela.

Emilia: ¿Por qué tienes que escribírsela?

David: Maria Cristina necesita unas informaciones que solamente nuestra abuelita sabe.

Emilia: ¿Cómo?

David: Maria Cristina quiere saberlas para su clase de historia.

Emilia: ¿Qué está haciendo en la clase de historia?

David: Está estudiando los años veinte. Quiere saber como era la vida entonces.

Emilia: Ah, comprendo. La abuelita puede decírselas porque sabe mucho de esta epoca.

David: Por supuesto.

Emilia: ¿Por qué Maria Cristina no escribe a la abuelita?

David: Porque quiero recibir cinco dólares de Maria Cristina.

Emilia: ¿Ella te la paga por escribir?

David: Naturalmente. La abuelita me ama más que Maria Cristina.

Emilia: Eres tonto. Nos ama lo mismo.

David: Ya lo sé. Pero Maria Cristina no lo piensa.

Emilia: ¡Hermanos!

Translation – A deception

David: I have to write a letter to our grandmother.

Emilia: Why do you have to write it to her?

David: Maria Cristina needs some facts that only
            our grandmother knows.

Emilia: What?

David: Maria Christina wants to know them for her
            history class.

Emilia: What are they doing in history class?

David: They are studying the twenties. She wants
            to know how life was then.

Emilia: Oh, I understand. Grandma knows a lot about that time period.

David: Of course.

Emilia: Why isn't Maria Cristina writing to grandmother?

David: Because I want to get five dollars from Maria Cristina.

Emilia: She is paying you five dollars for writing it?

David: Naturally. Grandma loves me more than Maria Cristina.

Emilia: You are silly. Grandma loves us all the same.

David: I know it. But Maria Cristina doesn't think so.

Emilia: Brothers!

Look at the dialogue and translate the following phrases.

3.1   a. tienes que escribírsela _____

          b. quiere saberlas _____

          c. puede decírselas_____

          d. te la paga por escribir _____

          e. nos ama _____

          f. lo sé _____

          g. no lo piensa _____

Complete this activity.

3.2   Practice the conversation several times and then share with your class.

✔ Adult check _____
                            Initial   Date

Double Object Pronouns

Double object pronouns are used to replace both the direct and indirect objects. To do this we place the indirect object pronoun (which usually refers to a person) before the direct object pronoun (which usually refers to a thing).

 Observe:

Paco me da el regalo.	Paco gives me the gift.
What does Paco give?	the gift – direct object – lo
To whom does he give it?	me – indirect object – me
Paco me lo da.	Paco gives it to me.

 Direct object pronouns:

me	me	**nos**	us
te	you	**os**	you
lo	it, him, you	**los**	them, you
la	it, her, you	**las**	them, you

 Indirect object pronouns:

me	to me	**nos**	to us
te	to you	**os**	to you
le (se)	to him, her, you	**les (se)**	to them, to you

Note that there is a **se** in parentheses after **le**. This is because when the direct and indirect object are in the third person (**lo, la, los, las** and **le, les**) the **le** and **les** change to **se** when using both direct and indirect object pronouns.

16

Examples:

Paco se los trae.	Paco is bringing them to him/her/you/them.
Nts. se la damos.	We are giving it to him/her/you/them.
Me la escribe.	He is writing it to me.
Te los preparan.	They are preparing them for you.
Nos la terminas.	You are finishing it for us.

The same happens as in the direct object and indirect object pronouns used singularly. If you need clarification in the third person you may add **a él, a ella, a Ud., a ellos, a ellas, a Uds.** after the verb form.

Se los vendo a él.	I am selling them to him.
Se lo traes a ellos.	She is bringing it to them.
Manuel se la escribe a Uds.	Manuel is writing it to you.

Rewrite the sentence, placing both the direct and indirect object pronoun in the sentence.

3.3   a. Juan vende el coche a Luis.

     b. Escribo una carta a mi amiga.

     c. Traemos los libros a Ana.

     d. La profesora explica la lección a Jorge.

     e. Los chicos describen el accidente al policia.

     f. Envio los regalos a mis abuelos.

     g. Pagamos la cuenta al camarero.

     h. Enseñas las lecciones a los alumnos.

     i. La madre lee el cuento a su hijo.

     j. Muestran las fotos a los amigos.

Double Object Pronouns With the Infinitive or Present Participle

With the infinitive the double object pronouns are attached to the end of the infinitive. When doing this it is necessary to put a written accent on the vowel of the **-ar, -er,** or **-ir** infinitive form.

Examples:

| **Tengo que vendérselo.** | I have to sell it to him/her/you/them. |
| **Vamos a escribírsela.** | We are going to write it to him/her/you/them. |

You may clarify here by adding the **a él, a ella, a Ud., a ellos, a ellas, a Uds.** at the end.

| **Puedo dárselos a Uds.** | I can give them to you. |
| **Deseas traérsela a ella.** | You want to bring it to her. |

With the present participle the double object pronouns are attached to the end of the present participle. When doing this it is necessary to put a written accent on **e** of the **-iendo** or the **a** of the **-ando** endings.

Examples:

| **Estoy vendiéndotela.** | I am selling it to you. |
| **Están enviándonoslo.** | They are sending it to us. |

 Rewrite the following sentences, replacing both objects with the correct pronouns and attaching them to the infinitive or present participle.

3.4

a. La profesora está explicando el problema a Jorge.

b. Tenemos que devolver el libro a Ana.

c. Mario y Luis están describiendo su viaje a sus amigos.

d. Debo enviar la carta a mi padre.

e. Prefieres enseñar las matemáticas a los estudiantes.

f. Prometen prestarme el dinero.

g. Estoy dandote las ideas.

h. Están mostrandonos las fotos ahora.

i. Quiero preparar la salsa para Uds.

j. Estás pagandome la cuenta.

SELF TEST 3

3.01   **In the following sentences underline the direct and indirect objects, labeling them above with D for direct and I for indirect.** (8 pts. each)

     1. Mario explica la idea a su amigo.

     2. El hombre vende su coche a la mujer.

     3. No escribo a Pablo esta carta.

     4. Tienes que dar al profesor tu examen.

     5. Estamos prestando el dinero a nuestro hijo.

3.02   **Rewrite the following sentences, replacing both the direct and indirect objects with pronouns and placing them in the correct position for that sentence.** (8 pts. each)

     1. Juan vende su bicicleta a José.

     2. Prefiero dar a Gregorio el dinero.

     3. Está explicando las direcciones al cliente.

     4. Doy el regalo a mi amigo.

     5. Escribes las noticias a tu abuela.

3.03   **Translate to English.** (4 pts. each)

     1. Tenemos que dárselo a él.

     2. Me los traen.

     3. Te las explicamos.

     4. Nos lo muestras.

     5. Están describiéndosela a ellas.

Score   _____

Teacher check   _____

                  Initial   Date

IV. PREPOSITIONAL PRONOUNS

Conversación – ¿Dónde está...?

La madre: No puedo encontrar los anteojos.
La chica: Están encima de la cabeza.
La madre: ¡Ay de mí! Ahora, ¿dónde está la bolsa?
La chica: Está al lado del sillón.
La madre: Ah, sí, al lado de él. Usualmente está dentro de él.
La chica: ¿Dónde están mis zapatos de tenis?
La madre: Están delante de la cama.
La chica: Usualmente están debajo de ella.
La madre: Y de vez en cuando, encima de ella.
La chica: Tienes razón, mamá.

Translation – Where is...?

Mother: I can't find my glasses.
Girl: They are on top of your head.
Mother: Oh, my. Now, where is my purse?
Girl: It's next to the armchair.
Mother: Oh, yes, next to it. It is usually in it.
Girl: Where are my sneakers?
Mother: They are in front of your bed.
Girl: Usually they are under it.
Mother: And once in a while, on top of it.
Girl: You're right, Mom.

Notice in this conversation that we have replaced the prepositional nouns with a pronoun. This helps the conversation flow more smoothly. After prepositions there are certain pronouns that are used as the objects. They are:

mí	me	**nosotros/nosotras**	us
ti	you	**vosotros/vosotras**	us
él	him, it	**ellos**	them
ella	her, it	**ellas**	them (feminine only)
usted	you	**ustedes**	you
sí	himself, herself, yourself, themselves, yourselves.		

Notice that with the exception of the **mí** and **ti**, the forms are the same as the subject pronouns. Note that **mí** requires an accent to keep it from getting confused with **mi** which means "my." Also when using **él**, the contraction is not made. The contraction is only made with **el** ("the," without the accent).

These pronouns are used after all prepositions requiring a pronoun. The following is a refresher list of common prepositions.

a	at, to	**de**	of, from
en	in, on	**por**	through
cerca de	near, close to	**detrás de**	behind
lejos de	far from	**a través de**	across from
al lado de	next to, beside	**encima de**	on top of, above
frente a	facing	**debajo de**	under, beneath
enfrente de	in front of	**dentro de**	inside, within
sobre	over, above	**delante de**	in front of
entre	between, among		

To this list you may add the following prepositions:

sin   without   **para**   for, in order to   **con**   with

Note: When combining **con** with **mí**, **ti** or **sí** there is a change:

con + mí = conmigo   with me
con + ti = contigo   with you
con + sí = consigo   with him(self), with her(self), with your(self), with them(selves).

 Fill in the blank with the correct pronoun for the English equivalent.

4.1

a. (him) Está enfrente de _____

b. (us) Vive al lado de _____

c. (you) Trabajo cerca de _____

d. (me) Vas sin _____

e. (them) Trabajo con _____

f. (you) Está cerca de _____

g. (her) Me siento a través de _____

h. (me) Lo pone detrás de _____

i. (us) Nos hablamos entre _____

j. (it, m.) Viven lejos de _____

Translate the following prepositional phrases.

4.2

    a. behind him _____

    b. among us _____

    c. next to you _____

    d. with me_____

    e. from her _____

    f. in front of them_____

    g. to us _____

    h. for it (f) _____

    i. on top of them_____

    j. on you _____

SPANISH

O N E

LIFEPAC 9
TEST

81 / 101

Name _____

Date _____

Score _____

SPANISH I: LIFEPAC TEST 9

1. Translate the following pronoun to Spanish and rewrite the sentence, placing it in the proper location. (5 pts. each)

   a. (him)   Traigo un libro.

   b. (you, s, fam)   Paco da un regalo excelente.

   c. (us)   Escribes una carta.

   d. (me)   Uds. muestran las fotos.

   e. (them, m.)   No quiero decir la razón.

2. Rewrite the following sentences, replacing the objects with pronouns. (5 pts. each)

   a. Decimos la verdad al profesor. _____

   b. Traigo las bebidas a mis amigos. _____

   c. Muestras el billete a tu padre. _____

   d. Escriben las noticias a nuestra familia. _____

   e. Da el regalo a su novia. _____

3. Translate to Spanish. (3 pts. each)

   a. with me   _____

   b. in front of her _____

   c. next to them (m) _____

   d. on top of it (f) _____

   e. without us   _____

4. Fill in the passage with one of the idioms from the list. Each will be used only once. (2 pts. each)

en punto por supuesto con permiso

en seguida a pesar de con frecuencia

en voz alta de esta manera con mucho gusto

de nuevo

Tenemos que salir _____ porque la fiesta comienza a las ocho _____ .

_____ estamos tarde. _____ , no quiero estar tarde

_____ . Mi hermana siempre nos grita _____ , "Uds. siempre

llegan tarde _____ saber la hora que comienza la fiesta." Y le respondo

_____ que tiene razón. Le pido a ella "_____" y ella me respondo

"_____" porque nos amamos mucho.

5. Write the name of the shop where the following items are sold. (2 pts. each)

a. pollo, biftec, puerco _____

b. papel, sobres, cuadernos _____

c. queso, mantequilla, leche _____

d. zapatos, botas _____

e. manzanas, peras, cerisas, fresas _____

f. aspirinas, medecinas _____

g. revistas, libros _____

h. flores, regalitos _____

Complete this activity.

4.3 Look at the following pictures and write where the ball is sitting in relationship to the people in the picture. Remember to use the correct preposition and the correct pronoun.

a.

b.

c.

d.

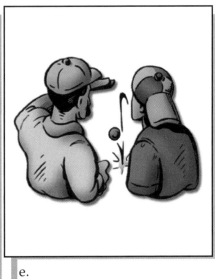

e.

f.

g.

h.

23

SELF TEST 4

4.01 **Translate the following phrases.** (2 pts. each)

a. next to him _____

b. with me _____

c. in front of them _____

d. from us _____

e. between you _____

f. far from her _____

g. under it (m) _____

h. on top of it (f) _____

i. at you _____

j. near me _____

4.02 **Look at the picture of the following people and answer the questions accordingly.** (10 pts. each)

1. ¿Dónde está Ana?

2. ¿Dónde está Paco?

3. ¿Dónde está José en relación a Ana?

Luis   Paco   José

Ana   Pilar   Elena

4.03 **Look at the pictures of the ball (la pelota) and write one sentence describing its location in relation to the box (la caja).** (10 pts. each)

a. _____

b. _____

c. _____

d. _____

e. _____

V. REVIEW AND USE OF IDIOMS

Conversación – ¿Una lección difícil?

En la clase de español.

El profesor:	A causa de sus actitudes, vamos a trabajar en lugar de jugar.
Paco:	Con permiso, por lo general hay solamente uno o dos que son malos. ¿Por qué todos tienen que sufrir?
El profesor:	De nuevo, todos no saben la lección de memoria. A pesar de tener suficiente tiempo para aprenderla, nadie puede hacerla.
Paco:	La podemos hacer en voz baja, pero en voz alta nos hace nerviosos.
El profesor:	Por supuesto, pero es necesario conquistar los nervios. Por eso vamos a practicar a menudo. Vamos a comenzar: A es para animal, B es para…
Paco en voz baja:	Es loco. Ya sabemos el alfabeto.

Translation – A difficult lesson?

The teacher:	Because of your attitudes, we are going to work instead of play.
Paco:	Excuse me, generally there are only one or two that are bad. Why do all have to suffer?
The teacher:	Again, everyone doesn't know the lesson by heart. In spite of having sufficient time to learn it, no one can do it.
Paco:	We can do it in low voice but out loud makes us nervous.
The teacher:	Of course, but it is necessary to conquer the nerves. Therefore we are going to practice often. Let's begin "A is for animal, B is for…
Paco, in a low voice:	He's crazy. We already know the alphabet

> **Look at the translation and write the meaning of the following phrases.**

5.1
a. a causa de_____

b. en lugar de_____

c. con permiso_____

d. por lo general _____

e. de nuevo _____

f. de memoria _____

g. a pesar de _____

h. en voz baja_____

i. en voz alta _____

j. por supuesto _____

k. por eso_____

25

Miscellaneous Idioms Using Prepositions

Often prepositions are used in helping express an idiomatic idea. Below are several that use common prepositions. These will help your writing and conversation by adding to the normal flow.

Those using a:

a casa	home
a causa de	because of, on account of
al + infinitive	on, upon
a menudo	often
a pesar de	in spite of

Those using de:

de esta manera	in this way
de memoria	by heart
de moda	in style
de nuevo	again
de repente	suddenly

Those using en:

en casa	at home
en lugar de	instead of
en punto	exactly
en seguida	at once
en voz alta (baja)	aloud, on a loud voice (in a low voice)

Those using con:

con frecuencia	frequently
con mucho gusto	gladly
con permiso	excuse me

Those using por:

por eso	therefore
por fin	finally
por lo general	generally
por supuesto	of course
por todas partes	everywhere

Answer the following questions using a prepositional idiom in your answer.

5.2

a. ¿Cómo vas a terminar este proyecto?_____

b. ¿Cuántas veces va tu madre a la carnicería?_____

c. ¿Por qué no viajas a Puerto Rico._____

d. ¿Quién puede ayudarme? _____

e. ¿A qué hora abre la librería? _____

f. ¿Dónde quiere Ud. sentarse? _____

g. ¿Cuándo llegan sus amigos? _____

h. ¿Dónde puede ver las montañas? _____

i. ¿Quién quiere leer? _____

j. ¿Qué es eso? _____

Conversación – En la librería

Yolanda: Necesito un libro sobre la historia de España en seguida.

Timoteo: ¿Por qué?

Yolanda: Tengo que hacer un reportaje en voz alta mañana.

Timoteo: De nuevo esperas hasta el fin.

Yolanda: Sí y no tengo tiempo para hacerlo de memoria.

Timoteo: Puedo ayudarte con mucho gusto.

Yolanda: Por supuesto. Podemos hacerlo de esta manera.

Timoteo: No, solamente puedo ayudarte encontrar un libro.

Yolanda: Con permiso. ¡Qué amigo!

Complete this activity.

5.3   Practice the conversation several times and then share with your class.

✔ Adult check _____
Initial   Date

Preguntas

Refer to the above conversation to answer the questions in complete Spanish sentences.

5.4   1. ¿Qué necesita Yolanda?

2. ¿Qué tiene que hacer?

3. ¿Por qué Timoteo parece frustrado?

4. ¿Qué ofrece hacer Timoteo?

5. ¿Cómo va a ayudarla?

> **Fill in the blanks in the following passage with a word from the vocabulary list.**

5.4   Vamos a la carnicería _____. Mi madre quiere la carne

_____ pescado. _____ comemos la carne en lunes y el

pescado en el martes. _____ nos gusta comer el arroz con pollo.

Al llegar a la carnicería decidimos comprar el jamón _____ su precio bajo.

Parece delicioso.

Conversation Practice.

> **Create a conversation using the following guidelines.**

5.5

A. Ask what your friend often does on Saturdays.

B. Respond with something you generally do.

A. Reply that you like the same thing.

B. Ask your friend to go with you.

A. Respond that gladly.

B. Say that you leave at exactly _____ o'clock.

A. Reply that of course you will be on time.

B. Say goodbye.

✔ Adult check _____

Initial   Date

SELF TEST 5

5.01 **Match the idiom with its meaning.** (5 pts. each)

_____ 1. por supuesto   a. at home

_____ 2. con permiso   b. because of

_____ 3. en casa   c. of course

_____ 4. de nuevo   d. excuse me

_____ 5. a causa de   e. again

5.02 **Match the idiom with its meaning.** (5 pts. each)

_____ 1. por todas partes   a. everywhere

_____ 2. con mucho gusto   b. in place of

_____ 3. en lugar de   c. in spite of

_____ 4. de repente   d. suddenly

_____ 5. a pesar de   e. gladly

5.03 **Give the English for the following idioms.** (5 pts. each)

a. a casa   _____

b. de esta manera   _____

c. en seguida   _____

d. con frecuencia   _____

e. por fin   _____

5.04 **Give the Spanish for the following.** (5 pts. each)

a. generally   _____

b. aloud, in a loud voice   _____

c. in style   _____

d. upon, on   _____

e. therefore   _____

$\frac{80}{100}$

Score _____

Teacher check _____
                                    Initial   Date

VI. CULTURE: LIFE IN SPAIN

A. History

Spain is rich in culture. It has been inhabited over the years by different ethnic groups which have contributed greatly to its variety. The first recorded inhabitants of Spain were the Iberians and the Celts. They were followed by the Phoenicians and the Greeks from the 11th to the 8th centuries B.C. The Carthaginians then invaded in the 3rd century B.C.

The Romans then invaded about 200 B.C. and ruled the nation for nearly six centuries. During their stay in Spain the Romans build bridges, roads and aqueducts. The most famous of the aqueducts is the one in Segovia which still carries water. It was built without using mortar.

The Visigoths defeated the Romans in the early 400's A.D. But they were defeated by the Moors who invaded Spain in 711 A.D. and remained in power for nearly seven centuries. They were driven out in 1492, the same year Columbus discovered the new world. The Moors provided Spain with the knowledge of philosophy, science, math, commerce and agriculture.

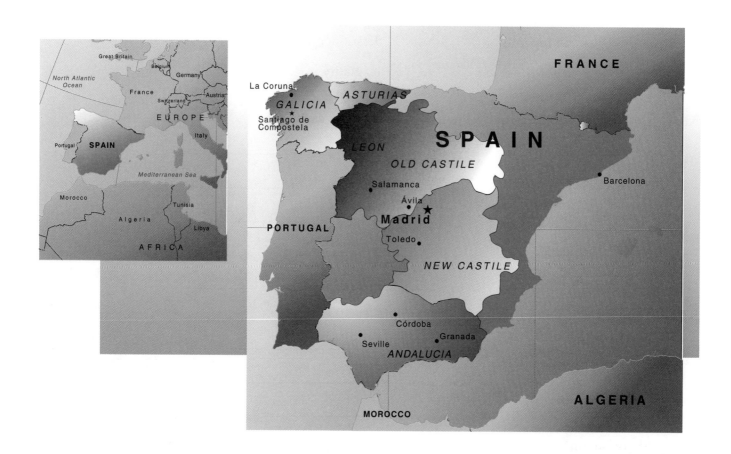

B. Regions of Spain

Spain has been divided over the centuries into fifteen regions. At one time they were separate kingdoms. Each of these regions is known for its own culture much like the variations in the United States in our states or regions.

Andalucía in the south of Spain is one of the largest regions. This region is noted for the flamenco dance, the raising of bulls for the bullfight, the production of sherry and the buildings built by the Moors. It also has three main cities: Granada, Córdoba and Seville, which was host to Expo '92.

Cordoba

Galicia is in the northwest, north of Portugal. The people of this region are very independent and consider themselves different than the Spaniards of Madrid, Seville or other parts of Spain. This region is noted for its fishermen and wood products. It is home to cities such as La Coruña, a port, and Santiago de Compostela with its famous church.

León is in the north central region of Spain. This region is famous for its Catholic monasteries and convents which helped train Catholic missionaries at the time of New World expansion.

Salamanca

Salamanca Cathedral

University of Salamanca

Salamanca is one of the main cities of this region. It is known for its impressive cathedral as well as its university, the oldest in Spain (founded in 1230). Salamanca is also known for La Casa de las Conchas, or "shell house." This house has shell designs on its outside walls.

Castile is in the central region of Spain. It is really two regions: Old Castile and New Castile. This region is where Madrid is located and also the home of the national language, Castilian, which is what we call Spanish. This area is a plain and therefore can be rather arid.

Avila

Avila is a walled city in this region. The entire old city is surrounded by imposing stone walls built to protect the city from invasion. Toledo is another city in this region. It was the first capital of Spain prior to it being moved to Madrid. It is famous for its metalwork such as steel and delicate jewelry.

Asturias is located along the northern coast of Spain. This region is noted for its talented sailors, mines and processing plants. This area of Spain is not a main tourist attraction but offers a look at the daily life of the Spanish. Its people are hardworking, rugged individuals who take pride in their work.

Toledo

C. Small Town Life

Spain is fortunate to have both large cities and small towns. The small town in Spain is set around a central square called the Plaza. At one end of the Plaza is the Catholic church, at another is the government building and around are found the small shops. In many of the small towns the women still shop daily or every other day for their food. It is customary to visit each shop, purchase what is necessary, converse a bit and move to the next shop. On Sundays many families go to the Plaza for a family walk and time to visit with neighbors and friends. This area is the central hub for the village. Homes in the rural area often have patios with extensive flower gardens and pots. Wrought iron gates decorate the windows and entry ways.

D. City Life

Many of the larger cities are very much like the cities in the United States. Madrid, for example, has an extensive mass transit system of buses, subways and taxis. In the large cities the people generally live in apartments. Curiously, most of the apartments have balconies decorated with pots of flowers, a carry over from rural life. In many areas of the large cities new construction has made small communities with all necessary services within that area.

Madrid Metro

Three customs of both city and rural life are the **paseo**, the **tertulia** and the **siesta**. The **paseo** is the term used by the Spanish when they go "strolling" which could almost be considered a nationl pastime. There are many parks and benches for people to rest and chat with friends and family. The **tertulia** is the custom of meeting with friends, usually in a small café and discussing topics of interest such as soccer or politics and enjoying the conversation and refreshment. The **siesta** is the afternoon nap time. While in some areas due to industrial and commercial development the siesta is being abandoned, it is still enjoyed by many. It is customary in Spanish society to have the large daily meal midday and a small supper in the evening. After the large meal, the Spanish people take a nap or rest period. Often in areas you will see that shops close from approximately one to four in the afternoon for the siesta.

Identify the place, people or event being described.

6.1

a. This region of Spain is north of Portugal and is noted for its fishermen and wood products.

b. These people inhabited Spain for over seven hundred years from 711 until 1492.

c. This is the central focus of a Spanish small town.

d. People enjoy this time together to discuss such topics as soccer or politics.

e. This region is really two regions, the old and the new, and is where Madrid is located.

f. This is the Spanish name for strolling.

g. The University of Salamanca is located in this region.

h. Besides the small shops, these are the two other buildings located around the plaza in a small Spanish town.

i. The region where they dance the flamenco and raise the bulls for bullfighting.

j. The region of Spain noted for its sailors, mines and processing plants.

SELF TEST 6

6.01   **Match the region with its location.** (6 pts. each)

_____ 1. Andalucía   a. north of Portugal

_____ 2. León   b. central Spain

_____ 3. Castile   c. northern coast of Spain

_____ 4. Galicia   d. southern Spain

_____ 5. Asturias   e. north central Spain

6.02   **Match the fact with its description.** (6 pts. each)

_____ 1. siesta   a. discussions and refreshments

_____ 2. tertulia   b. the number of regions in Spain

_____ 3. paseo   c. strolling

_____ 4. Moors   d. the afternoon nap

_____ 5. fifteen   e. the people that invaded Spain in 711

6.03   **Essay questions – answer with facts.** (20 pts. each)

a. Describe a small town in Spain.

b. Describe a large city in Spain

VII. COMPREHENSION, WRITING AND CONVERSATION

Let's Read

Miguel y Ana van al centro de la ciudad. Quieren ir de compras. Van a tener una fiesta de cumpleaños para su madre. Van a la carnicería para comprar la carne. Entonces a la frutería para las frutas para una ensalada. Después van a la papelería para las decoraciones. Y la heladería para el helado. Y finalmente a la pastelería para un pastel delicioso. Los dos van a preparar la comida. Mientras están preparando la comida, Miguel pregunta a Ana si tiene el regalo. Ana responde que Miguel tiene el regalo. El dice que no. Ay, ¡qué problema! No tienen un regalo. Rápidamente Miguel corre a la librería y compra un libro de jardines y flores que a su madre, por supuesto, le va a gustar.

A las siete toda su familia está en casa y llegan unos amigos. Su madre está muy sorprendida por la fiesta. Todos comen bien y cantan mucho. Es una fiesta maravillosa. A su madre le gusta mucho el libro. Miguel y Ana están contentos.

 Refer to the paragraph above to answer the following questions.

7.1   a. ¿Por qué van al centro?

      b. ¿Qué necesitan?

      c. ¿Cuáles tiendas visitan?

      d. ¿Qué es el problema?

      e. ¿Adónde corre Miguel?

      f. ¿Qué compra?

      g. ¿Quiénes asisten a la fiesta?

      h. ¿Cómo es la fiesta?

      i. ¿Le gusta el libro a su madre?

      j. ¿Cómo están Miguel y Ana?

Let's Write

Answer the following general questions in complete Spanish sentences.

7.2
    a. ¿Quién vive al lado de su casa?

    b. ¿Dónde pones los libros?

    c. ¿Cuándo vas a salir?

    d. ¿Dónde está la heladería?

    e. ¿Cómo van a presentar el reportaje?

    f. ¿Quién me da el libro?

    g. ¿Dónde va a dejarte?

    h. ¿Qué quiere Luis darle?

    i. ¿Cuánto dinero te da su padre?

    j. ¿Quién les vende el coche?

Rewrite the following sentences using double object pronouns to replace the objects.

7.3
    a. María da una carta a Luis.

    b. Nts. traemos las bebidas a nuestros amigos.

    c. Paco me prepare una cena especial.

    d. Yo te traje un regalo.

    e. Muestras las fotos a Joaquín.

    f. Vamos a preparar las lecciones para la profesora.

    g. Tienes que mostrarme tu proyecto.

    h. Quiere decirnos la verdad.

    i. Estamos mostrando el coche nuevo a nuestros amigos.

    j. Está diciendo la respuesta al profesor.

Let's Listen

Listen to the following paragraphs which will be read twice, then answer the questions about each paragraph.

7.4   1. ¿Adónde van? _____
     a. a la escuela   b. a la librería   c. a la casa de Unamuno

      2. ¿Qué tipos de libros necesitan? _____
     a. de autores españoles   b. de autores ingleses   c. del Sr. Sanchez

7.5   1. ¿ Adónde van? _____
     a. al mercado   b. a la frutería   c. al centro

      2. ¿Qué quiere Miguel? _____
     a. helado   b. zapatos   c. nada

      3. ¿Qué compran para las madres? _____
     a. flores   b. zapatos   c. pastel

7.6   1. ¿Qué hacen los tres amigos. _____
     a. preparan para una fiesta   b. visitan amigos   c. comen

      2. ¿Qué les gusta hacer a Mario y Tomás? _____
     a. cocinar   b. hablar   c. limpiar y arreglar

7.7   1. ¿Cómo tienen que leer? _____
     a. silente   b. en voz baja   c. en voz alta

      2. ¿Cómo son los estudiantes? _____
     a. nerviosos   b. agradables   c. hambrientes

      3. ¿De qué habla Maria? _____
     a. su visita a un pueblo español   b. la panadería   c. el restaurante

Let's Speak

Prepare a conversation using the following guidelines. Try to include the "extra" words that help conversations flow.

7.8   You and a friend are deciding what to do for the day.

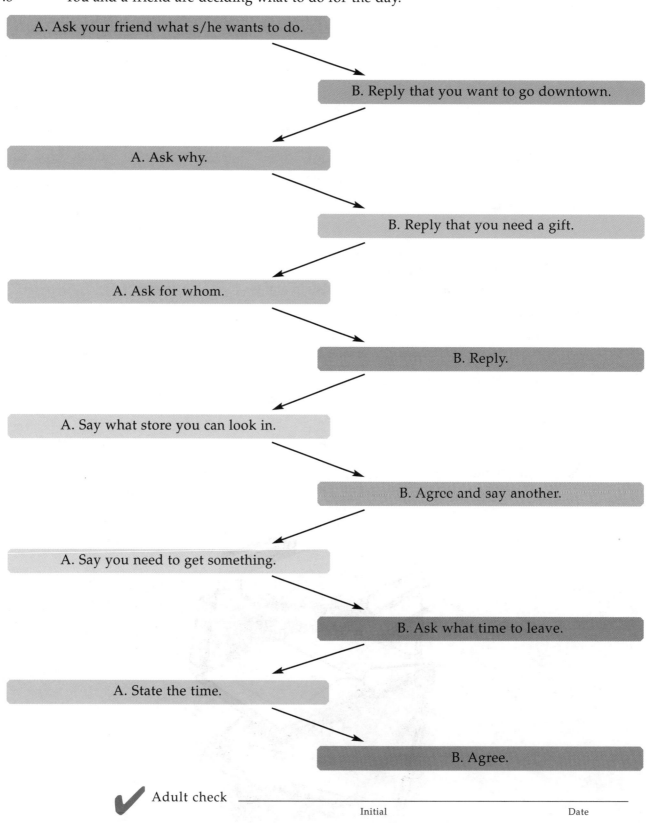

A. Ask your friend what s/he wants to do.

B. Reply that you want to go downtown.

A. Ask why.

B. Reply that you need a gift.

A. Ask for whom.

B. Reply.

A. Say what store you can look in.

B. Agree and say another.

A. Say you need to get something.

B. Ask what time to leave.

A. State the time.

B. Agree.

✔ Adult check _____
                    Initial   Date

Note: This section does not have a Self Test.

VIII. REVIEW AND COMPARISONS

Direct Object Pronouns

Remember the eight direct object pronouns:

me	me	**nos**	us
te	you	**os**	you (Spain)
lo	him, you, it	**los**	them
la	her, you, it	**las**	them (fem. only)

Translate to English the following sentences.

8.1   a. Lo veo. _____

b. Me ayudas. _____

c. No nos dicen. _____

d. Puedo visitarte. _____

e. Las quieren. _____

Translate to Spanish the following sentences.

8.2   a. We have them (m). _____

b. They bring me water. _____

c. I am going to write you. _____

d. You see her. _____

e. She needs it (f). _____

The Present Progressive Tense

Remember the present progressive tense is formed by using the correct form of **estar** and the present participle (**-ando**/**-iendo**). This tense is used to emphasize the fact that the action is in progress.

Translate to English.

8.3   a. Estoy trabajando hoy. _____

b. Estamos escribiendo las lecciones. _____

c. Estás diciendo la verdad. _____

d. Están yendo a la dulcería. _____

e. Paco está jugando el fútbol. _____

Translate to Spanish.

8.4   a. I am thinking about them._____

        b. We are taking the bus._____

        c. She is living here. _____

        d. You (pl) are leaving now. _____

        e. You (s) are sleeping. _____

Comparisons

Comparisons are made between two similar things:

I am taller than you.

This movie is more interesting than that one.

This house is smaller than our old one.

To express the comparison in Spanish the formula is **más** or **menos** + **adjective** + **que**.

Paco es más alto que Luis.

Esta clase es menos aburrida que la clase de historia.

 Translate to English.

8.5   a. Pablo es más inteligente que Arturo.

        b. Este autobús es más nuevo que ese autobús.

        c. Ese tren es más rápido que el otro.

        d. Mi bicileta es menos grande que la tuya.

        e. Su coche parece menos nuevo que el mío.

 Translate to Spanish.

8.6   a. Mike is shorter than you.

        b. School is harder than soccer.

        c. History is less boring than English.

        d. Planes are faster than trains.

        e. Bikes are slower than cars.

Superlatives

This formula is used when comparing part to a whole.

Bill is the tallest in the family.

People are smarter than animals.

The formula for doing this is **article +más/menos + noun + adjective + de**.

Guillermo es el más alto de la familia.

 Translate to English.

8.7
    a. Español es la más fácil de las lenguas.

    b. Los aviones son los más rápidos de los transportes.

    c. España tiene las playas más bonitas del mundo.

    d. Rosas son las mejores de las flores.

    e. El basquetbol es el más emocionante de los deportes.

 Translate to Spanish.

8.8
    a. I am the blondest in my family.

    b. My brother is the best soccer player in the school.

    c. New York is the largest city in the US.

    d. Tennis is the most popular sport in our school.

    e. This book is the least interesting in the library.

Note: This section does not have a Self Test.

Vocabulario: El pueblo

la carnicería	the butcher shop	el carnicero	the butcher
la dulcería	the candy shop	el dulcero	the confectioner
la farmacía	the pharmacy	el farmacéutico	the pharmacist
la florería	the flower shop	el florero	the florist
la frutería	the fruit store	el frutero	the fruit vendor
la heladería	the ice cream shop	helar (ie)	to freeze
la lechería	the dairy store	el lechero	the milkman
la librería	the book store	el librero	the book vendor
el mercado	the market	el mercadero	the merchant
la panadería	the bakery	el panadero	the baker
la papelería	the stationary shop	el papelero	the paper merchant
la pastelería	the pastry shop	el pastelero	the pastry chef
la zapatería	the shoe store	el zapatero	the shoe maker

Prepositions:

a	at, to	por	through
en	in, on	detrás de	behind
cerca de	near, close to	a través de	across from
lejos de	far from	encima de	on top of, above
al lado de	next to, beside	debajo de	under, beneath
frente a	facing	dentro de	inside, within
enfrente de	in front of	delante de	in front of
sobre	over, above		
entre	between, among		
de	of, from		

Miscellaneous Prepositional Idioms:

Those using a:

a casa	home
a causa de	because of, on account of
al + infinitive	on, upon
a menudo	often
a pesar de	in spite of

Those using de:

de esta manera	in this way
de memoria	by heart
de moda	in style
de nuevo	again
de repente	suddenly

Those using en:

en casa	at home
en lugar de	instead of
en punto	exactly
en seguida	at once
en voz alta (baja)	aloud, on a loud voice (in a low voice)

Those using con:

con frecuencia	frequently
con mucho gusto	gladly
con permiso	excuse me

Those using por:

por eso	therefore
por fin	finally
por lo general	generally
por supuesto	of course
por todas partes	everywhere